Contents

MARY SLESSOR

1848–1915

CHRISTIAN HEROES: THEN & NOW

MARY SLESSOR

Unit Study

Curriculum Guide

JANET & GEOFF BENGE

YWAM PUBLISHING
A Ministry Of Youth With A Mission
P.O. Box 55787, Seattle, WA 98155

YWAM Publishing is the publishing ministry of Youth With A Mission. Youth With A Mission (YWAM) is an international missionary organization of Christians from many denominations dedicated to presenting Jesus Christ to this generation. To this end, YWAM has focused its efforts in three main areas: 1) training and equipping believers for their part in fulfilling the Great Commission (Matthew 28:19); 2) personal evangelism; 3) mercy ministry (medical and relief work).

For a free catalog of books and materials write or call:
YWAM Publishing
P.O. Box 55787, Seattle, WA 98155
(425) 771-1153 or (800) 922-2143
www.ywampublishing.com

Mary Slessor: A Unit Study Curriculum Guide

10 09 08 07 06 05 04 03 02 10 9 8 7 6 5 4 3 2 1

Published by Youth With A Mission Publishing
P.O. Box 55787
Seattle, WA 98155

ISBN 1-57658-253-1

Printed in Germany.

Introduction

Mary Slessor: A Unit Study Curriculum Guide

This unit study guide is designed to accompany the book *Mary Slessor: Forward into Calabar* from the Christian Heroes: Then & Now series by Janet and Geoff Benge. It provides the Christian school teacher and homeschooling parent with ways to use the book as a vehicle for teaching or reinforcing various curriculum areas, including

- Creative writing.
- Drama.
- Movie critiquing.
- Reading comprehension.
- Essay writing.
- History and geography concepts.

As there are more ideas than could possibly be used in one unit, it is the parent/teacher's job to sift through the ideas and select those that best fit the needs of the students.

The activities recommended in this unit study guide are

- Reflective of a wide range of learning styles.
- Designed for both group and individual study.
- Suitable for a range of grade levels and abilities.

Learning Styles

Choose those activities that are best suited to your student or students. For example, when studying the physical features of a country, a kinesthetic learner will learn best by producing a three-dimensional clay model representing the physical features of the country, whereas a visual learner will find it more meaningful to produce a poster map of the country for the classroom wall.

Group or Individual Study

While the activities contained in this unit study guide are designed to be carried out by a student working alone, instructions are provided for adapting an activity for a group.

Grade Levels/Abilities

As you thumb through this unit study guide, you will note that grade levels are not assigned to particular activities, though some areas, essay topics for example, progress from the simple to the complex. This approach has been taken because students of varying grade levels can undertake most of the activities. For example, one of the activities asks students to research and write an essay that traces the history of malaria and current treatment of the disease. A fourth grader doing this activity might simply say that the disease is caused by mosquitoes whereas a ninth grader undertaking the same assignment would be able to say more specifically that it is caused by microscopic protozoa carried by mosquitoes and transmitted during their bite. Each student uses the same activity and instructions to create work appropriate to his or her age and cognitive ability.

In the center of this unit study guide you will find two foldout pages. These pages contain three maps and a fact sheet to be filled out by the student. The maps and fact sheet are designed to be photocopied onto individual pages so that each student can store them in his or her folder. They are for use with the social studies section of this unit study guide (chapter 6).

Before you begin teaching from this unit study guide, please read through each section. You may wish to highlight the activities that appeal to you or that you know your students would enjoy or be challenged by. Many teachers find it useful to plan the culminating event (see chapter 8) first and then select a range of learning activities that lend themselves to this event.

For the sake of brevity in the instructions that accompany each section, the word *teacher* includes the homeschooling parent, and the word *student* refers to a child either in a traditional classroom or in a homeschool environment.

1

Key Bible Verses

The authors have selected four Bible passages that can be used alongside or as part of this unit study. For your convenience, these verses have been quoted in two versions: the King James Version and the New International Version. Of course, many other appropriate Bible verses can be added to the list if more are needed. One selection is from the Psalms since the text says (page 98) that to keep from startling wild animals, Mary often sang hymns while clapping her hands and stomping her feet as she walked through the jungle. The verses can be used in a number of ways. Four ideas for using them are listed below.

Memorization. The teacher can assign one or all of the verses to be memorized during the duration of the study. A chart could be made to track which students have completed memorizing which verses.

Meaning. The verses can be used to spark conversation on the spiritual aspects of Mary's life. This can then be translated into action by having students form groups and present one of the verses to the class in a creative manner. Students could make up a skit to illustrate the meaning of the verse or present a one-act play to show how the verse was relevant in the life of Mary Slessor.

Devotional. The teacher might also consider beginning a class or family devotional book. To do this, the teacher should familiarize the students with a variety of devotional writings and then ask them to write a devotion based upon their understanding of one of the verses as it relates to the life of Mary Slessor. The pages could then be glued or copied into a blank book, illustrated, and signed. The various devotions could be read aloud at appropriate times, including during assemblies and family devotional times and at the culminating event.

Display. Students could design a plaque, wall hanging, or banner with one of the verses written on it. This could be hung in a prominent place while the unit study is undertaken and used for decoration during the culminating event.

"Have not I commanded thee? Be strong and of a good courage; be not afraid, neither be thou dismayed: for the LORD thy God is with thee whithersoever thou goest" (Joshua 1:9 KJV).

"Have I not commanded you? Be strong and courageous. Do not be terrified; do not be discouraged, for the LORD your God will be with you wherever you go" (Joshua 1:9 NIV).

“Set your affection on things above, not on things on the earth” (Colossians 3:2 KJV).

“Set your minds on things above, not on earthly things” (Colossians 3:2 NIV).

“And he saw also a certain poor widow casting in thither two mites. And he said, ‘Of a truth I say unto you, that this poor widow hath cast in more than they all: For all these have of their abundance cast in unto the offerings of God: but she of her penury hath cast in all the living that she had” (Luke 21:2–4 KJV).

“He also saw a poor widow put in two very small copper coins. ‘I tell you the truth,’ he said, ‘this poor widow has put in more than all the others. All these people gave their gifts out of their wealth; but she out of her poverty put in all she had to live on” (Luke 21:2–4 NIV).

“I will love thee, O LORD, my strength. The LORD is my rock, and my fortress, and my deliverer; my God, my strength, in whom I will trust; my buckler, and the horn of my salvation, and my high tower. I will call upon the LORD, who is worthy to be praised: so shall I be saved from mine enemies” (Psalm 18:1–3 KJV).

“I love you, O LORD, my strength. The LORD is my rock, my fortress and my deliverer; my God is my rock, in whom I take refuge. He is my shield and the horn of my salvation, my stronghold. I call to the LORD, who is worthy of praise, and I am saved from my enemies" (Psalm 18:1–3 NIV).

2

Display Corner

Many students will enjoy collecting and displaying objects from the country and culture they are studying. It is motivational to designate a corner of the room, including a table or desk and wall space, that can be used for this purpose. Keep some index cards on the table and encourage students to label their contributions, including as much information as possible about where each object came from, what it is used for, and who would use it.

Encourage students to ask their parents and friends if they have anything interesting (but not valuable) from Africa that they could bring to class. A visit to an import shop could also yield some very interesting display items, as would a trip to the local library to find books on Africa and famous African people and events. Following is a list of things students (or you) might like to display. Of course, there are many more options.

- A large map of Africa
- Items of African art, including masks, sculptures, textiles, and woodcarvings
- Articles or books about David Livingstone or Henry Stanley
- Information about slavery (or human rights in general)
- A game of Mancala, a widely available African game
- African food and food-related items, such as oranges, lemons, cassava, bananas or plantains, and vegetables such as yams
- Examples of African writing. Bibles and tracts are available through the American Bible Society at (800) 32-BIBLE or www.americanbible.org
- Photographs and articles about Africa, both in the past and in the present
- African stamps and coins
- Dolls in national dress
- Articles and photographs about Nigerian wildlife, such as monkeys, jackals, hippos, elephants, and lions
- Newspaper articles about Nigeria or Southwestern Africa that highlight current events in the various regions of the country
- Brightly colored cotton textile products
- The flags of the Federal Republic of Nigeria, Cameroon, and other African countries

3

Chapter Questions

There are four questions related to each chapter of *Mary Slessor: Forward into Calabar*:

1. A vocabulary question drawn from the text and referenced to a page in the book
2. A factual question arising from the text
3. A question to gauge the level of a student's comprehension
4. An open-ended question seeking an opinion or interpretation

These questions are designed for students to complete on their own. They are best answered after a student finishes reading each chapter in the book. Answers to the first three questions for each chapter are given in Appendix B of this guide. The answer to the fourth question is open-ended and needs to be evaluated separately. Since question four deals with a student's interpretation or opinions, it is a good question on which to base a group discussion. Keep in mind that there is no right or wrong answer to question four, only positions a student needs to justify.

To gain maximum benefit from the questions, the students should write full-sentence answers, not just one or two words. For example, in response to the question, "To what city did Mary's family move when she was eleven years old?" students should write, "Mary's family moved to the city of Dundee when she was eleven years old," not just "Dundee."

Each vocabulary question asks the students to use the new word in a sentence. If you ask them to do this, make sure their sentences clearly demonstrate the meaning of the vocabulary word.

A supplement to answering the questions is to have students write a short summary of each chapter or write a response to the chapter in their journal. This could involve the students' writing about how they relate to Mary Slessor's actions, noting whether this is how they think they would react in a similar situation, and speculating as to what might happen next in the story.

Chapter One

1. What is a rebuttal (page 12)? Use the word in a sentence.
2. What was unique about Mary Slessor's hair?
3. Why did Mary let all the parties involved in a dispute "talk until they could talk no more"?
4. Do you think Mary made the right decision when she ordered Okpono's brother-in-law to whip Okpono? What would you have done? Why?

Chapter Two

1. What does founded mean (page 20)? Use the word in a sentence.

2. To what city did Mary's family move when she was eleven years old?
3. Why was the inside temperature of the mill kept between eighty and ninety degrees Fahrenheit?
4. Many people in nineteenth-century Scotland could not read. How do you think your life would be different if you could not read?

Chapter Three

1. What does drudgery mean (page 37)? Use the word in a sentence.
2. To which place did Mary promise never to go alone?
3. Why did Mary feel "many different emotions" at her father's funeral?
4. What do we learn about Mary's character from the way she behaved when she was threatened by the teenage boys?

Chapter Four

1. What does chided mean (page 44)? Use the word in a sentence.
2. What was the name of the town in Calabar where the missionary compound was located?
3. Why did Mary want to go to Calabar even though she knew it was considered the most dangerous missionary post?
4. Mary left for Africa on July 30, 1876. What are some of the things you think she would miss about living in Scotland?

Chapter Five

1. What does dissuade mean (page 62)? Use the word in a sentence.
2. Why was the engine on the *Ethiopia* turned off once they were at sea?
3. Why was Mary so upset when she learned about the English trading goods for alcohol?
4. Do you think the British were wrong to trade rum and gin with the Africans if that is what the Africans wanted? Why or why not?

Chapter Six

1. What is a furlough (page 65)? Use the word in a sentence.
2. Approximately how many natives attended the Sunday service in Duke Town during Mary's first week in Calabar?
3. How did Mary's walk through Duke Town make her begin to see that being a missionary in Calabar was not going to be as easy as she had thought?
4. Imagine that you walked with Mary and Mrs. Sutherland through the streets of Duke Town to visit the family mourning their son's death, the brides in the fattening hut, and the widows of the rich man. What are some of the thoughts that might run through your head? What else would you want to know about Efik people?

Chapter Seven

1. What does illiterate mean (page 85)? Use the word in a sentence.

2. What did Mary do when she mistook the bright moonlight for sunlight?
3. Why was Mary so disappointed to go home to Scotland after three years in Calabar?
4. Mary was invited to be the honored guest of King Eyo at his banquet. If you were Mary, what one thing would you most like to discuss with the king? Why?

Chapter Eight

1. What does itinerated mean (page 89)? Use the word in a sentence.
2. What usually happened to twins that were born in Calabar?
3. What was the main reason Mary decided to live like a native in Old Town?
4. Do you think it was wise or morally right for the British to destroy Old Town after Chief Willy died? Why or why not?

Chapter Nine

1. What does commotion mean (page 105)? Use the word in a sentence.
2. What was unique about how Mary slept in Ibaka?
3. Why did King Eyo try to dissuade Mary from visiting Chief Okon at Ibaka?
4. What was one character trait Mary displayed when she insisted on speaking to the men of Ibaka on behalf of the young wives who had disgraced their husbands? Was this trait important to Mary's missionary work overall? Why or why not?

Chapter Ten

1. What is a hammock (page 111)? Use the word in a sentence.
2. How far inland did Samuel Edgerley explore before his death?
3. Why did Mary insist that Janie had to travel with her even though Mary was very ill?
4. Do you think Mary felt differently the second time she returned home on furlough? Why or why not? Use examples from the text to support your argument.

Chapter Eleven

1. What is an inhabitant (page 125)? Use the word in a sentence.
2. What was the Zenana Scheme?
3. What change in circumstances led the missionaries to ask the British consul for permission to go farther inland?
4. Why do you think Mary wanted so desperately to go inland to the Okoyong region, when her life was already very challenging?

Chapter Twelve

1. What does undaunted mean (page 135)? Use the word in a sentence.
2. When Mary returned to Ekenge, she found it deserted. Why?
3. When Mary and the children first arrived in Ekenge, why was she unable to get them warmed up?
4. Mary was often more able than the male missionaries to get the African men to do what she asked. Why do you think that was true?

Chapter Thirteen

1. What does glistening mean (page 142)? Use the word in a sentence.
2. Why did Mary strip down to her slip as she hurried through the jungle?
3. What message were the tribal leaders sending to their people when they burned Ekpa with oil?
4. When Mary saved the life of their chief, some of the village women told Mary, "You will always be our mother, and we will be your children." Why do you think a statement like that was so meaningful to Mary?

Chapter Fourteen

1. What does menacingly mean (page 154)? Use the word in a sentence.
2. What did Mary's new name *Eka Kpukpru Owo* mean?
3. Why did Mary think of the bully in Dundee when she confronted the warrior with the oil-filled ladle?
4. What do you think would be some of the worst aspects of living in a culture ruled by superstitions?

Chapter Fifteen

1. What does surveyed mean (page 163)? Use the word in a sentence.
2. Why was a smoky fire lit inside a new hut before it was inhabited?
3. Why was Mary's plan to save the hostages dependent on the missionaries' arriving from Duke Town in time?

4. Do you think the hostages accepted that it was their fate was to be killed? Why or why not?

Chapter Sixteen

1. What is a delegation (page 179)? Use the word in a sentence.
2. How was the message of the new treaty with the coastal tribes passed on to other tribes in the area?
3. Which did Mary view as more important: her call to live at Ekenge or her engagement to Charles Morrison?
4. When Mary was appointed vice-consul of Okoyong, she had the power to enforce or forbid any local practices. Why do you suppose Mary allowed the people of Ekenge to continue some of their superstitious practices?

Chapter Seventeen

1. What is an epidemic (page 193)? Use the word in a sentence.
2. What was Mary's reaction when the new hospital in Itu was named the Mary Slessor Mission Hospital?
3. What was the last thing Mary did to honor Chief Edem?
4. Looking back over Mary's life, why do you think she was able to thrive where other missionaries were not even able to survive?

4

Student Explorations

Student explorations are a variety of activities that are appropriate to a wide range of learning styles. These activities consist of the following:

Essay Questions. These are questions that can be used as essay writing ideas. Students can either be assigned a topic or choose their own from the list. The simplest essay topics appear first, followed in order by those that are more complex.

Creative Writing. This includes writing such things as newspaper articles, poems, letters, résumés, songs, and journals.

Hands-on Projects. These are various kinds of projects, such as charts and graphs, models, comic strips, family crests, mottoes, dioramas, book covers, and mobiles.

Audio/Visual Projects. These involve such things as using a tape recorder to conduct a mock interview or to produce a radio play or commercial, or using still and video cameras to create dramatic presentations.

Arts and Crafts. These include art forms and craft forms used in Africa and Great Britain.

Language Examples. Some examples of words written in the Efik language are given. While Mary spoke Efik, this is not a major Nigerian language (the national language of Nigeria is English). Students can use them to make banners or place mats for the culminating event or in their hands-on projects. For example, they could use a phrase to decorate a postcard sent home by Mary.

[Note on group projects: All the suggestions described below are individual learning activities. However, some of the activities have bracketed paragraphs like this one after them that offer suggestions on how the activity can be adapted for class or group use.]

Essay Questions

1. Mary faced many challenges growing up. Discuss some of the ways in which her upbringing may have shaped her ability to adapt to missionary life in Calabar.

2. During Mary's lifetime, malaria was a very dangerous sickness, especially in swampy, tropical areas. Research and write an essay that traces the history of malaria and discusses current treatment of the disease.

3. Mary was a strong woman who eventually became known as *Eka Kpukpru Owo*, the Mother of Us All. Describe some of the challenges she faced as a single female missionary and some of the innovative ways she overcame them.

4. David Livingstone was a great inspiration to Mary.

Research his life and compare and contrast the lives of these two very influential missionaries.

Creative Writing

1. Mary's walk through Duke Town with Mrs. Sutherland just two weeks after arriving in Calabar made a strong impression on her. Write a letter from Mary to her mother shortly after this walk through town.
2. The Foreign Mission Board decided to build a mission hospital in Calabar, and they named it the Mary Slessor Mission Hospital. Write a persuasive letter from the board member who suggested the name, outlining the reasons why he or she felt Mary deserved to have a hospital named after her.
3. Write a newspaper article about Mary's experience of being harassed by the gang of boys in the Pends. Be sure to include the amazing conclusion to the story.
4. Imagine you are Mary Slessor. Write a letter to Queen Victoria explaining why you feel alcohol should not be used to trade with African tribes.
5. Write a poem about Mary's joy and anticipation after finding out that she would be going to Calabar, a place she referred to as a post of honor.
6. Imagine that you are Mary. Write a series of journal entries about your first trip from Scotland to Calabar.

Hands-on Projects

1. Write and illustrate a children's book that covers some or all of the aspects of Mary Slessor's life.
2. Make a model of the mission house and medical dispensary at Ekenge built by Charles Ovens.
3. Before she left for Calabar, Mary toured Edinburgh with two other future missionaries also named Mary. Make a poster advertising the visit of the "Three Marys" to your church.
4. Make a diorama of an important event in Mary Slessor's life, such as Etim's funeral or when she stood up to the Okoyong warrior.
   [Coordinate the dioramas of several students to represent key events in Mary's life. A tape-recorded commentary could be added to the exhibit.]
5. Use a Venn diagram to illustrate similarities and differences between Mary's life in Dundee and her life in Calabar.
6. Music is very important in African culture. Research and listen to some African music, then design a colorful CD cover that would be appropriate for the music.

Audio/Visual Projects

1. Using a video camera, make a production of *Mary Slessor, This Is Your Life*. Think carefully about whom to invite to participate in the show and what they might say about Mary. Be sure to have them remind her of memorable moments.

2. Write a short documentary of Mary Slessor's life. Using a video camera, record yourself as the narrator. Include an audio recording of Mary speaking Efik, available online at http://www.dundeecity.gov.uk. (Click on Leisure Time, then Libraries, then Central Library, then search for Mary Slessor.)

3. Imagine that you were a member of the mission board that interviewed Mary for her first missionary post in Calabar. Write and ask the questions, recording the interview with a tape recorder or video camera.
   [This can be done as a group project, by having several students portraying members of the mission board and one student acting as Mary.]

Arts and Crafts

1. Masks are a common African art form. These masks often represent good and evil characteristics. Create and decorate a mask that represents Mary's practical love for the people of Calabar.

2. Mary worked in a textile mill. Study the process of making fabric from wool. Design your own African-style textile project (the Yoruba are well known for their brightly colored fabrics).

3. Mary loved to knit. It soothed her nerves and helped those around her feel at ease. Learn to knit something simple.
   [Have members of the class knit squares. Sew these together to form a blanket. Give the blanket to a needy cause.]

4. The next section gives several examples of words written in the Efik language. Use these words to

make banners, posters, and bookmarks, and use them on invitations or place mats for the culminating event.

Language Examples

God is love.
Abasi edi ima.

Pray for Nigeria.
Bong akam no Nigeria.

Jesus said, "I am the light of the world."
Ami ndi uyai erenbot.

5

Community Links

Many communities have a rich supply of people and places to which students can be exposed to help them learn about and appreciate other cultures. It is well worth the effort to find out what your community has to offer with regard to the unit you are studying. For example, you may know people who are foster parents or who have adopted children. You may also live near a university attended by international students from Africa.

While it would be wonderful if you could take a field trip to visit some of these people and places, if you can't, it is often possible to have visitors come to the classroom. Whether you decide to take a field trip or invite a guest to your classroom, such activities need to be flanked by sound educational choices. Otherwise much of the educational value of the event will not be realized. The following three steps will help students derive the greatest educational value from a field trip or classroom visit.

Step One: Preparation

Students should always research the topic before they begin a classroom interview or field trip. In doing so, they will be ready to ask intelligent questions based upon a sound knowledge of their topic. For example, if the students are going to interview a person from Nigeria, they should know beforehand some of the major cultural groups in Nigeria and be aware of the vast differences that exist within the country. With this in mind, they can ask questions that zero in on Ibibio Ekpo culture compared with the Hausa or Fulani of northern Nigeria. They can ask questions such as: Why are masks so important to the Ibibio? What is the principal artwork of the Yoruba? How can it be that English is the national language of Nigeria?

As the teacher, you need to give the students a clear idea as to why they are going on a field trip and what they are expected to produce with their findings. For example, you might say to them, "We are going to a museum to see a collection of African art. When we get back, I want you each to list five different types of artwork you saw and locate the region where they originated on a map of Africa."

Students should be encouraged to compile lists of questions they want answers to, based upon what they have already learned. They should carry a clipboard with them to write down answers, draw sketches, and note observations. (For less motivated students, a simple worksheet of activities to be completed on the field trip itself can be a good idea.) Such activities reinforce the idea that the field trip is a serious educational event and that the student is there to gather information, not just to be a sightseer.

Step Two: The Event

During the field trip or classroom visit, make sure that the students remain on task. Insist that they be respectful of property and other people at all times. Make sure that you have a spokesperson designated to thank whomever you talk to as well as the parents who help with the event.

Step Three: Processing and Reflection

Students should be given time to process the information they have gathered from their field trip or classroom visit and reflect on it, both individually and as a class. This can take many forms, including making flow charts or diagrams of what they have learned, editing interviews for articles or audiovisual presentations, writing reports, and making booklets. Something as simple as a class book called *Did You Know?*, in which each student writes down one fact he or she learned from the field trip, can serve as an effective reflection tool.

Suggested Community Links

African People. Ordinary people are some of the best resources of all. Perhaps there are some students from Africa at a nearby university or a family from Africa in your neighborhood. For example, you could invite a member of the family to address the class so that students can learn about the family's history. How long has the person or family been in the United States? What country or part of Africa are they from? What language did they speak in Africa and would they write or speak something in their language?

What types of food does the family eat at home? What customs do they still practice in America?

African Drum and Dance Group. Many cities have an African drum and dance group that you could invite to your school or that you could visit. It would be very helpful to schedule a time to visit when students would have a chance to ask questions and learn about the songs and instruments from members of the group.

Day Care. Visit a day care with your students to learn about all the tasks that must be carried out when looking after babies and small children. Have the students make a list of all the things Mary had to do for the children in her care.

Retired Missionaries. Ask around to see if you can find a retired missionary who has worked in Africa. If so, invite him or her to speak to your class. Ask the person to bring any artifacts he or she has and dress in national costume, if possible. This will make the visit more memorable for the students.

A Place for People in Crisis or Need. Mary Slessor always tried to help those in need, especially those who needed emergency medical care. Choose an institution or ministry working with people in need in your community and have a class fundraiser to raise money for it. Then either take the class to the institution or ministry or have one of its representatives come to the class to accept your gift. For example, you might contact a shelter for battered women or a foster home near you. Find out what it needs, and work with the class to find a way to meet one of those needs. The gift doesn't have to be large. A toaster or a child's car seat or even used items such as children's books and toys may be needed. You could also invite an emergency medical technician, doctor, or nurse to talk with the class about giving emergency first aid.

6

Social Studies

The social studies section is divided into five categories, each with suggestions on how to use the material given. The categories are briefly described below.

Places. This section covers significant places related to the story and named in the text of the book *Mary Slessor: Forward into Calabar*.

Journey. This category covers Mary Slessor's journey from Scotland to Calabar.

Terms/Vocabulary. This section gives ideas for studying some of the terms used in the book.

Geographical Characteristics. This section contains suggestions for mapping some of the physical characteristics of Nigeria.

Conceptual Questions. This section provides the teacher with conceptual social studies questions related to the book.

Places

These places are categorized by region, with the page number where they are first referred to in the book given in parentheses. Students can undertake a range of activities with these place names. They can

- Locate and mark the places on the relevant map. (Maps for this purpose are located in the foldout map section of this guide.)
- Note other points, such as their absolute location (latitude and longitude), and then observe how this location compares to other locations mentioned in the book. For example, calculate which location is closer to the equator or the North Pole.
- Calculate the relative locations of various places mentioned in the book. For example, how far is it from Duke Town to Creek Town or from Dundee to Liverpool?
- Construct a key to show population density in Nigeria.
- Explore how some of the place names have changed since the time of the story and give reasons for such changes.
- Pinpoint the places on a large wall map in the classroom. Students can then use index cards to write explanations as to why the various places are mentioned in the story. Each card could be pinned to the wall with a length of yarn connecting it to the appropriate place on the map.

Places in the United Kingdom

Dundee (14)
Scotland (14)
Aberdeen (16)
Gilcomston (16)
Southampton (39)
Edinburgh (45)
Liverpool (51)
Downfield (91)
Devon (116)

Places in Africa

Duke Town (46)
Old Town (47)
Creek Town (47)
Eknetu (47)
Okofiorong (47)
Qua (94)
Akim (94)
Ibaka (98)
Atam (111)
Cameroon (125)
Ekenge (131)
Ifako (153)
Kuri (170)
Akpap (191)
Arochuku (196)

Journey

Using the following journey, students can

- Map the journey on the relevant map.
- Where possible, add details to the map from the story, such as how long each part of the journey took, when Mary started and finished the journey, and the kinds of transportation she used along the way.
- Compare the journey Mary took to taking the same journey today. Students could research how they might reach this destination today, how long it would take to get there, and how much it would cost.

Mary's journey

Mary visited or traveled near the following places on her journey from Scotland to Calabar:

Dundee (49)
Liverpool (51)
Mersey River (52)
Irish Sea (53)
Atlantic Ocean (53)
Cape Verde (57)
Sierra Leone (57)
Ivory Coast (57)
Nigeria (57)
Calabar (57)
Cross River (59)
Parrot Island (59)
Calabar River (60)
Duke Town (61)

Terms/Vocabulary

Following is a list of terms used in the book. The page number where the term is first used is given in parentheses. The list covers a range of terms from the simple to the advanced. Students can use this list to

- Define and memorize the terms. You may find it helpful to asterisk or highlight in some way those terms you think would be appropriate for your students. If they know the meaning of all but five of the terms, have them learn only those five. Conversely, if they are unfamiliar with most of the terms, choose a realistic number for each student to explore and learn.
- Produce an individual or class reference book of terms. Assign each student a number of terms to write definitions for or draw sketches of. From this research, a book of definitions can be made, with one page allotted for each definition. This book could be added to throughout the year. (Students may need a dictionary to help them here.)

- Play reinforcement games such as *Go Fish*. To do this, draw some of the sketched definitions from the list compiled in the preceding point onto index cards and have students take turns pairing them with written definitions.

Terms/vocabulary

customs (12)
region (12)
disputes (12)
industrialization (17)
tenement (18)
slum (18)
natives (32)
colony (46)
territories (46)
headwind (53)
currency (55)
settlements (56)
horizon (57)
coastline (58)
river channel (59)
grove (61)
shrine (72)
Victorian (78)
civilization (82)
delta (98)
tributary (98)
spheres of influence (124)
superstitions (138)
torrents (148)
delegation (179)
trading goods (180)
barter (181)
representative (186)
harvests (191)

Geographical Characteristics

Have students use an atlas to locate the following and then mark them on the blank map of Nigeria from the foldout map section in the center of the book:

- The following seven rivers in Nigeria, their sources, and courses: the Niger, Benue, Kaduna, Sokoto, Komadugu Gana, Cross, and Calabar
- The thirty-six Nigerian states
- The four major cultural regions: Yoruba, Hausa, Fulani, and Ibo
- The four major geographical regions: the Coastal

Belt, Jos Plateau, the Savanna, and Adamawa Plateau
- Lake Chad and Kainji Lake
- The six largest cities in Nigeria
- The latitude and longitude lines that bisect Nigeria
- The two climatic zones of Nigeria
- The seas and oceans that border Nigeria: the Gulf of Guinea, Bight of Benin, Bight of Biafra and the Atlantic Ocean
- The countries Nigeria shares borders with: Benin, Niger, Chad, and Cameroon
- Vogel Peak (Dimlang), the highest peak in Nigeria

Conceptual Questions

The following questions are ordered from the simple to the complex. Using these questions, you could ask students to

- Write one or more paragraphs to answer each question.
- Present an oral report to the class on one of the questions.
- Discuss the answer(s) to a question or questions in a group context.

Questions to ponder

1. Locate and name two countries in the world that are larger than Nigeria, two that are about the same size, and two countries that are smaller.
2. How large is Nigeria compared to the United States?

3. What is the population of Nigeria compared to the population of the United States?
4. Study a physical map of Nigeria. Where do you think most of the population would live? Why? Use a population map to test your hypothesis. Were you right or wrong? Why?
5. Nigeria is the most heavily populated country in Africa. Use a population density map to find other countries that are also heavily populated. What do these countries have in common?
6. Find a map that shows known oil and natural gas deposits in Nigeria. How much crude oil and natural gas are mined each year in Nigeria? How does this compare with oil and natural gas production in other parts of the world?
7. Write a paper explaining why this statement is true: "Many of the countries with some of the richest natural resources also have the lowest per capita incomes and poorest standards of living."

7

Related Themes to Explore

Any unit study has natural links to many other topics that can also be explored. While it is impossible to pursue all such links in this context, the spoke diagram on the next page shows some related topics that students might find interesting to study alongside Mary Slessor.

There are two ways you might integrate some of these links into your classroom. Some teachers and parents have the flexibility to be able to choose the topics their students study and even alter their selections partway through the year. If you are able to do this, use the theme wheel to help identify other topics you might like to follow up this unit with. For example, after studying Mary Slessor, your class might become interested in other Westerners who had the desire to explore inland Africa.

Other teachers and parents are locked into a less flexible curriculum. If this is your situation, you may still have the ability to change the order in which various topics are taught. Look through the topics listed to see whether any coincide with topics you have already scheduled for later in the year. Consider the possibility of scheduling the teaching of these topics closer to this unit so that cross-curriculum learning can take place.

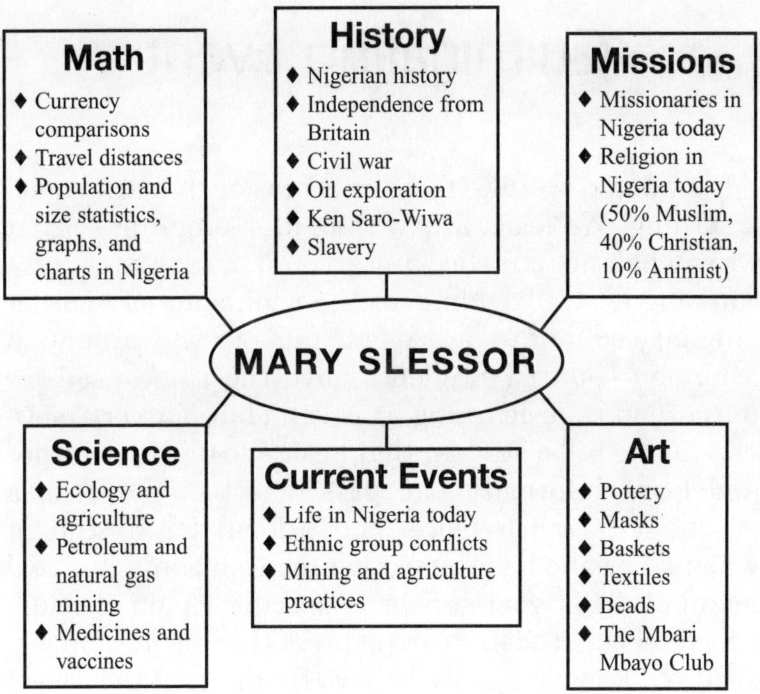

8

Culminating Event

As adults, we like to have a reason to learn something. We learn a new computer program so that we can balance our checking account, a song so that we can sing it at a wedding, or the rudiments of another language so that we are able to find our way around in a foreign country. Students have the same need for purpose in their learning. It is valid but not very motivational to tell a student that he or she needs to gather and learn information to pass a test or move up a grade. It is much more motivational for a student when he or she has some other, more meaningful goal in mind. This goal can be a specific forum through which each student can express his or her newly acquired knowledge. We believe that part of the role of the teacher is to provide such a forum, which we will call the culminating event.

As the name implies, the culminating event marks the end of the unit study and gives a sense of closure to the topic. It also serves to put what students have learned into a larger context that can then be shared with others.

The culminating event can be as simple as inviting the class next door (or the homeschooled children down the street) to come and hear poems and stories and view the written work that students have completed. Conversely, it could be as involved as hosting a parent/neighborhood dinner featuring Nigerian food, songs, games, plays, and a presentation on the life and achievements of Mary Slessor.

No matter how simple or elaborate the culminating event is, make sure you have the broad outline of it in mind before planning the other activities for your unit study, as the two are integrally linked.

Idea Sparks

Food. Prepare and serve regional food. A wide variety of fruits and vegetables is eaten in Nigeria. Primary foods of Nigeria include yams, maize (corn), rice, and beans. The people also eat plantains (a kind of banana), oranges, bananas, and cassava. Nigerian food is often cooked in palm oil or peanut oil and is often seasoned with red peppers. Some Nigerian meals feature beef, chicken, fish, or lamb; however, most Nigerians do not eat much meat.

A traditional meal in a village would probably include rice, beans, and some sort of tuber (potato, yam, or cassava). No utensils are used; food is eaten with the hands. The same foods are typically eaten at every meal since there is not much distinction between meals. Fruits are common, though not often eaten during the meal. They are more commonly eaten as snacks throughout the day.

Music. Play traditional African music in the background to set the mood (many libraries stock ethnic music selections).

Oral Presentations. Present poems, essays, reports, speeches, reviews, and devotions that students have written during the course of the unit study.

Display. Display other work, including artwork, mapwork, models, newspapers, and video interviews.

Clothing. Younger students might enjoy dressing up in the traditional brightly colored clothing common to Nigeria. The 250 or so ethnic groups in Nigeria wear a wide range of clothing and hats. In the cities, many Nigerians wear Western-style clothing. But other city dwellers and most people in rural areas wear traditional clothing. Traditional garments for men and women include long, loose robes or shirts made of white or brightly colored fabrics. The men may also wear short, full jackets with shorts or trousers. Hats range from small round caps, often worn by men, to turbans, which are worn by men and women. Rural Nigerians in some parts of the country wear only a loincloth, a small piece of fabric tied around the waist.

Cultural Activities. Play traditional African children's games such as Mancala.

Appendix A

Books and Resources

This appendix is divided into six sections: (1) other biographies of Mary Slessor, (2) related books, (3) a related Christian Heroes: Then & Now book, (4) a related movie and documentary, (5) related articles from *National Geographic*, and (6) Internet sites.

Many books about Mary Slessor are written at a higher reading level than the books in the Christian Heroes: Then & Now series and would be interesting for a teacher to read for his or her own information and as background for the unit. Children learn best by example, so consider choosing one good adult book to read and enrich your own understanding of the topic. Resources for younger children are also included, and if they can be found, they can make it easy for younger family members or less able readers to participate in the unit study at their own level.

Some of the books listed here are more difficult to get copies of than others. If they are not available at your local Christian bookstore, many of the titles can be located in secondhand bookstores (try using the Internet to locate them). Most of the titles are also available through the national interlibrary loan service.

Other Biographies of Mary Slessor

All the biographies listed on the bibliography page of *Mary Slessor: Forward into Calabar,* as well as others that may be of interest, are listed here. Each listing has basic information on how to locate the book, including its ISBN. The approximate age level of the intended reader is also given, along with the number of pages in each book and some comments to help you decide whether you might want to include this book in your unit study.

TITLE: *The Missionary Heroine of Calabar: A Story of Mary Slessor*
Author: Esther E. Enock
Publisher: Pickering & Inglis, 1937
ISBN: N/A
Age Level: 8 years and up, 96 pages

Synopsis: This book gives a general overview of Mary Slessor's life.

Comments: This book is a reflection of the time period in which it was written. It tends to be overly dramatic and would not appeal to most students today.

TITLE: *Nigerian Pioneer: The Story of Mary Slessor*
Author: Ronald Syme
Publisher: William Morrow & Co., 1964
ISBN: N/A
Age Level: 8 years and up, 190 pages

Synopsis: This book also gives a general overview of Mary's life. It has pen and ink sketches throughout.

Comments: This book presents Mary's story in a clear and simple manner. It is written to a younger reader than *Mary Slessor: Forward into Calabar* and does not introduce any material that is not already covered there.

TITLE: *Mary Slessor of Calabar: Missionary Pioneer*
Author: W. P. Livingstone
Publisher: Zondervan Publishing House, 1984
ISBN: 0310274516
Age Level: Adult, 352 pages

Synopsis: This book covers every aspect of Mary's story in detail.

Comments: This is the definitive work on Mary Slessor, originally published by Hodder and Stoughton in 1915. It is written in a scholarly but interesting fashion. It contains approximately thirty photos of Mary and her work, along with two very detailed maps of her missionary territory. If you want more details about Mary's life, this would be the book to read.

TITLE: *God and One Redhead: Mary Slessor of Calabar*
Author: Carol Christian & Gladys Plummer
Publisher: Hodder and Stoughton, 1970
ISBN: 340129166
Age Level: Adult, 190 pages

Synopsis: This is a scholarly account of the life of Mary Slessor. It contains many long and interesting quotes from her contemporaries. It has a detailed map of the Lower Cross River region and eighteen photographs of Mary, her children, and her homes.

Comments: Both of the authors spent extensive amounts of time in Calabar, and Gladys Plummer was the superintendent of education there. They both knew many people who were familiar with Mary's work and the social conditions she battled. This first-hand knowledge shines through, making this book well worth reading.

TITLE: *Mary Slessor: Heroine of Calabar*
Author: Basil Miller
Publisher: Bethany House, 1985
ISBN: 0871238497
Age Level: Adult, 140 pages

Synopsis: This biography is weighted heavily towards Mary's work in Africa and spends very little time reviewing her childhood or the social conditions under which she grew up. It does not contain maps or photographs.

Comments: This book was first published over half a century ago in 1944 and it shows in the stilted language and preachy style. It would not appeal to young people.

TITLE: *Mary Slessor: Queen of Calabar*
Author: Sam Wellman
Publisher: Barbour Publishing Inc., 1998
ISBN: 157748178X
Age Level: Adult, easy reading, 208 pages

Synopsis: This general biography of Mary deals well with her childhood, but ends with the minute of her death. There is no commentary on her funeral or the lasting impact she has had on the West African Coast. It does not contain additional maps or photographs.

Comments: This book is an easy read, though it covers much of the same material as *Mary Slessor: Forward into Calabar*.

Related Books

Listed in this section are two other books that fit around the life of Mary Slessor. The listings include the ISBN, age level, and relevant comments.

Of course, there are many other books that relate in some way to this unit study. You may want to record inside the back cover of this unit study guide the titles of other books you find particularly helpful.

TITLE: *Travels in West Africa: The Classic Account of One Woman's Epic & Eccentric Journey in the 1890s*
Author: Mary Henrietta Kingsley
Publisher: Phoenix Press, 2001
ISBN: 1842121103
Age Level: 10 years and up, 304 pages

Synopsis: British explorer Mary Henrietta Kingsley explored and wrote about areas in Western Africa during the time of Mary Slessor. She landed in Calabar in 1893 and from there explored the Niger River and Cameroon and traveled as far south as Angola.

Comments: This book provides an interesting look into African exploration by a contemporary of Mary Slessor. There are several other books by and about Miss Kingsley.

TITLE: *Uncommon Traveler: Mary Kingsley in Africa*
Author: Don Brown
Publisher: Houghton Mifflin, 2000
ISBN: 0618002731
Age Level: 4–8 years, 32 pages

Synopsis: This book introduces the idea of African exploration to younger children.

Comments: While "the other Mary" was not a missionary, her journeys in Africa may be interesting for children and may give them a richer understanding of Mary Slessor's experience.

Related Christian Heroes: Then & Now Book

TITLE: *David Livingstone: Africa's Trailblazer*
Authors: Janet and Geoff Benge
Publisher: YWAM Publishing, 1999
ISBN: 1576581535
Age Level: 10 years and up, 216 pages

Comments: David Livingstone (1813–1873) was a missionary who became famous as an explorer. He mapped vast areas of inland Africa, became the first European to cross the continent west to east, and discovered numerous natural landforms, most notably the Victoria Falls.

Related Movie and Documentary

Listed in this section are a documentary and a movie that relate to the topic of Africa. As with all unfamiliar material, it would be prudent to preview them before showing them to the class.

Movies and documentaries are particularly useful in showing the visual details of another place and time period. As students watch, encourage them to study the clothing, weather, crops, terrain, and other geographical factors shown in the movie or documentary.

TITLE: Africa Series: *Western Region*
Publisher: Encyclopedia Britannica
Type: Documentary

Length: 20 minutes
Year: 1993

Comments: This documentary focuses on the sixteen countries between the Sahara Desert and the South Atlantic Ocean, with special attention given to Nigeria. Location, climate, vegetation, lifestyles, and economic activities are explored. This will serve as a good introduction to Nigeria for your students.

TITLE: *Out of Africa*
Director: Sydney Pollack
Author: Isak Dinesen
Starring: Meryl Streep, Robert Redford
Type: Movie, biographical drama
Length: 150 minutes
Year: 1985
Rating: PG

Comments: Many people consider this movie to be a classic. The movie is based on the memoirs of Karen Blixen, who established a coffee plantation in East Africa while her husband led a life of hunting and infidelities. The story follows her attempt to overcome female stereotypes during colonial times. This movie is definitely for older children, and the teacher should use discretion before showing it to students. You may want to show your students appropriate excerpts after carefully previewing the movie. The scenery is magnificent, and the movie may help to paint a broad picture of Africa for students.

Related National Geographic Articles

Many magazines contain articles related to this unit study. We have chosen to reference *National*

Geographic because it can provide contemporaneous commentary on many events, since it dates back to the 1880s, and because it is widely available in libraries and schools throughout the country.

These articles and their accompanying photographs represent just some of those available that bear on aspects of Mary Slessor's life. They can be used in a variety of ways to support and reinforce this unit study. For example, you could have students read the article "Beyond the Bight of Benin" (August 1959) and study the paintings. Then they could create their own painting of a Nigerian scene using similar elements to those used to illustrate the article. Likewise, students could read "Three-Wheeling Through Africa" (January 1934), research the route a modern motorcycling pair might take across Africa, and write a report. They could include projected travel times, stops, and costs involved.

Article about Dundee

TITLE: "Low Road, High Road, Around Dundee"
Issue Date: April 1936, pages 547–576

Description: This article gives a history of Dundee from the 1700s on. It includes many references to mills similar to the one where Mary worked. Contains photos and maps.

Articles about Nigeria

TITLE: "The New English Province of Northern Nigeria"
Issue Date: November 1904, pages 433–442

Description: This is an account of what British troops found when they seized the Nigerian city of Kano in 1903.

It is an interesting eyewitness account of Nigeria, contemporary with Mary Slessor. It does contain graphic descriptions of torture and other forms of human suffering.

TITLE: "Three-Wheeling Through Africa: Two Adventurers Cross the So-called Dark Continent North of Lake Chad on Motorcycles with Side Cars"
Issue Date: January 1934, pages 37–92

Description: Two young American men take five months to drive from Lagos to the Red Sea. This article is written in a lively and engaging style. Photos include seminudity.

TITLE: "Nigeria: From the Bight of Benin to Africa's Desert Sands"
Issue Date: May 1944, pages 537-568

Description: Explores the diversity of Nigeria's tribes and customs. Contains great photos.

TITLE: "Progress and Pageantry in Changing Nigeria"
Issue Date: September 1956, pages 325–365

Description: This is a written and photographic record of Queen Elizabeth II's visit to Nigeria. She was the first reigning British monarch to visit the colony, and she was met with much pomp and ceremony.

TITLE: "Beyond the Bight of Benin"
Issue Date: August 1959, pages 221–253

Description: This is a very interesting article written by a husband and wife who are artists. They travel across Nigeria and Cameroon painting pictures of the scenes and people they meet. They write a lot about the superstitious beliefs they encounter along the way.

TITLE: "The Niger: River of Sorrow, River of Hope"
Issue Date: August 1975, pages 152–189

Description: This article is about the path of the Niger River and the people and cultures along its banks. Contains photos with partial nudity.

TITLE: "Nigeria Struggles With Boom Times"
Issue Date: March 1979, pages 413–444

Description: Written nineteen years after independence, this article explores how Nigeria has struggled to raise its standard of living and deal with its legacy of colonialism, corruption, and civil strife. It has a large section on oil as a national resource. Contains photos, one of which is of a corpse.

Related Internet Sites

The websites listed here may have been updated since this guide was published and as a result may contain information not reviewed here. It is vital that you preview the sites before allowing your students to view them. General websites about Nigeria may contain links to political or interest websites that may be inappropriate for children.

www.dundeecity.gov.uk

This site contains great information about Mary from the City of Dundee Central Library. You can even listen to a recording of Mary speaking Efik. Click on Leisure Time, then Libraries, then Central Library, then search for Mary Slessor.

www.yoruba.org

This is a website devoted to the Yoruba ethnic group of western Nigeria. There are links to articles about Nigerian current events, as well as specific information about the Yoruba. However, the sight does not appear to be updated regularly so information may be out of date.

www.motherlandnigeria.com

This is a very comprehensive website with an education area and a kidzone that includes stories, games, music samples, and an introduction to several Nigerian languages.

www.nigeria.com

This website carries general, political, and business news about Nigeria, as well as current events and related links.

www.bs-nigeria.org

This is the website for the Bible Society of Nigeria, with information about current missions and the country itself.

Appendix B

Answers to Chapter Questions

Chapter One

1. A rebuttal is an opposing argument.
2. Mary Slessor had red hair.
3. Mary believed that if everyone with an interest in a dispute had an opportunity to "talk until they could talk no more," then they would be more likely to listen to her when she was ready to give her decision.

Chapter Two

1. Founded means to have started something, such as a club, business, or organization.
2. When she was eleven, Mary's family moved to Dundee, Scotland.
3. The mill owners kept the inside temperature of the mill between eighty and ninety degrees Fahrenheit because they believed the heat made the fabric finer.

Chapter Three

1. Drudgery means hard, dull work.
2. Mary promised never to go to the Pends alone.
3. Mary loved her father, and he was kind when he was not drunk. However, she was relieved that he wouldn't be able to spend the little money the family had on alcohol anymore and that the family wouldn't have to suffer his violent drunken rages.

Chapter Four

1. Chided means to have scolded for a fault or offense.
2. The missionary compound was located in Duke Town.
3. Mary wanted to go to Calabar despite the danger because she felt God needed her there most since so few missionaries were willing to go there.

Chapter Five

1. Dissuade means to convince not to do something.
2. The engine was turned off because the ship did not carry enough coal for the entire journey, and it had to sail part of the way.
3. Mary was upset to find that the British traded rum and gin with the natives because she knew from her own experience how destructive alcohol could be.

Chapter Six

1. A furlough is a vacation from duty.
2. Five or six hundred natives were in the service.
3. Mary saw the Africans in their own community and homes and realized that it would be difficult to get

the gospel message across to people whose lives were ruined by alcohol, superstitions, unhealthy customs, and poor living conditions.

Chapter Seven

1. Illiterate means unable to read and write.
2. Mary mistakenly rang the morning bell at 3 A.M. and woke up the others in the mission house.
3. Rather than going home with great stories of success, Mary felt that she was going home sick and defeated. She was wondering if she was doing any good in Calabar.

Chapter Eight

1. Itinerated means to have made a regular tour from place to place.
2. Twins born in Calabar were usually killed within hours of birth.
3. Mary wanted to save money to send home to her family.

Chapter Nine

1. Commotion is a noisy or violent disturbance.
2. Mary slept between two fattened and well-oiled wives of Chief Okon.
3. King Eyo was concerned for Mary's safety. He didn't trust Chief Okon, and the journey to Ibaka would be dangerous.

Chapter Ten

1. A hammock is a type of hanging bed or seat made of netting or canvas.

2. Samuel Edgerley explored 160 miles inland to Atam.
3. Mary was afraid that if she left Janie behind, Janie's relatives would try to kill her since they had already sent someone to Mary's hut to kill her twin brother.

Chapter Eleven

1. An inhabitant is a permanent resident of a place.
2. The Zenana Scheme was a plan of the Foreign Mission Board to allow female missionaries the freedom to work more independently from men.
3. The missionaries asked for permission to go farther inland when they heard that the British were planning to send in British troops and open up inland trade routes. The missionaries wanted to be the first to make contact with the inland tribes.

Chapter Twelve

1. Undaunted means not discouraged or fearful.
2. Ekenge was deserted because Chief Edem's mother had died earlier in the day and the entire village had gone to the funeral.
3. Mary was unable to warm them up because all of their clothing was wet, and so was the hut they were in.

Chapter Thirteen

1. Glistening means reflecting a sparkling light.
2. Mary took her outer clothes off because they were weighed down with mud and made walking difficult.
3. The tribal leaders were sending the message that it

was very dangerous for the people to have anything to do with Mary.

Chapter Fourteen

1. Menacingly means with an attitude of threatening to cause evil or harm.
2. *Eka Kpukpru Owo* means the Mother of Us All.
3. Mary thought of the bully in Dundee because he had also tried to frighten her, but she knew that she must not back down or show fear.

Chapter Fifteen

1. Surveyed means to have looked over in detail.
2. A fire was lit in a new hut to smoke out the bugs and to dry out the wood.
3. The Duke Town missionaries brought the magic lantern show to honor Etim. Mary hoped this great show of honor would make it unnecessary for the hostages to be buried with him.

Chapter Sixteen

1. A delegation is a group chosen to represent others.
2. The message was spread by the sound of drums.
3. Mary felt her call to live at Ekenge was more important than her engagement.

Chapter Seventeen

1. An epidemic is a rapid spread of a contagious disease in an area.
2. Mary was dismayed that the hospital was named after her.
3. Mary buried him.

Also from Janet and Geoff Benge...

More adventure-filled biographies for ages 10 to 100!

Christian Heroes: Then & Now

Gladys Aylward: The Adventure of a Lifetime • 1-57658-019-9
Nate Saint: On a Wing and a Prayer • 1-57658-017-2
Hudson Taylor: Deep in the Heart of China • 1-57658-016-4
Amy Carmichael: Rescuer of Precious Gems • 1-57658-018-0
Eric Liddell: Something Greater Than Gold • 1-57658-137-3
Corrie ten Boom: Keeper of the Angels' Den • 1-57658-136-5
William Carey: Obliged to Go • 1-57658-147-0
George Müller: The Guardian of Bristol's Orphans • 1-57658-145-4
Jim Elliot: One Great Purpose • 1-57658-146-2
Mary Slessor: Forward into Calabar • 1-57658-148-9
David Livingstone: Africa's Trailblazer • 1-57658-153-5
Betty Greene: Wings to Serve • 1-57658-152-7
Adoniram Judson: Bound for Burma • 1-57658-161-6
Cameron Townsend: Good News in Every Language • 1-57658-164-0
Jonathan Goforth: An Open Door in China • 1-57658-174-8
Lottie Moon: Giving Her All for China • 1-57658-188-8
John Williams: Messenger of Peace • 1-57658-256-6
William Booth: Soup, Soap, and Salvation • 1-57658-258-2
Rowland Bingham: Into Africa's Interior • 1-57658-282-5
Loren Cunningham: Into All the World • 1-57658-199-3

Heroes of History

George Washington Carver: From Slave to Scientist • 1-883002-78-8
Abraham Lincoln: A New Birth of Freedom • 1-883002-79-6
Meriwether Lewis: Off the Edge of the Map • 1-883002-80-X
George Washington: True Patriot • 1-883002-81-8
William Penn: Liberty and Justice for All • 1-883002-82-6
Harriet Tubman: Freedombound • 1-883002-90-7
John Adams: Independence Forever • 1-883002-51-6
Clara Barton: Courage under Fire • 1-883002-50-8

Unit Study Curriculum Guides are available for these biographies.

Heroes for Young Readers...

Introduce children to the exciting true stories of Christian heroes with rhyming text and vivid color illustrations! For ages 6 and up.

Author: Renee Taft Meloche • Illustrator: Bryan Pollard

Children, parents, and teachers love the adventurous Christian Heroes: Then and Now biographies and unit study curriculum guides. Now Heroes for Young Readers introduces younger children to the lives of Christian heroes! Whether reading for themselves or being read to, children love the captivating rhyming poems and unforgettable color illustrations of the Heroes for Young Readers series.

Gladys Aylward: Daring to Trust • 1-57658-228-0
Nate Saint: Heavenbound • 1-57658-229-9
Eric Liddell: Running for a Higher Prize • 1-57658-230-2
George Müller: Faith to Feed Ten Thousand • 1-57658-232-9
Amy Carmichael: Rescuing the Children • 1-57658-233-7
Mary Slessor: Courage in Africa • 1-57658-237-X
Corrie ten Boom: Shining in the Darkness • 1-57658-231-0
William Carey: Bearer of Good News • 1-57658-236-1

...and more coming soon!

Picture books all ages will treasure.
Hardcover editions!